Sisters:

Reflections
on Sisterhood

Sisters:

Reflections
on Sisterhood

Edited by Maureen Slattery

BARNES
&NOBLE
BOOKS
NEW YORK

This is for Lisa, Christine, Suzanne, Kathleen, Laura and, of course, Thomas.

The quotes in this book have been drawn from many sources, and are assumed to be accurate as quoted in their previously published forms. Although every effort has been made to verify the quotes and sources, the publisher cannot guarantee their perfect accuracy.

2003 Barnes & Noble Books

ISBN 0-7607-4073-9

Printed and bound in the United States of America

M9 8 7 6 5 4 3 2 1

NANCY: Sisters are a defense against life's cruel circumstances.
JESSICA: Sisters are life's cruel circumstances.

—NANCY AND JESSICA MITFORD

I GREW UP IN A FAMILY OF SISTERS, ACTUALLY, SIX girls and one boy. But the boy was last, and late, so I was raised largely in a world of women. Aspirations that many parents hold for their sons only were directed towards us, the daughters: doctor, lawyer, architect; they were all within our grasp. I could do anything I desired, as long as it wasn't what my sister wanted.

Anyone who has a sister will recognize the complex weave that holds together most sisters. For every story of undying devotion, there is a competing tale of wretched sibling rivalry. Here, you will find the ever-faithful Delany's along side the bickering Mitford girls; devoted Virginia and Vanessa follow Cinderella's wicked steps; and the competitive nuances of Jane Austen go up against the fidelity of the Brontës. Together, they show the range of emotions associated with being a sister.

As children, my sisters and I were equally pleased and horrified at being endlessly informed of our similarities and differences; an essentially reductive practice that left us "looking like," "acting like," or "being like" the very person from which we were most trying to distance ourselves. Indeed, for several years, my older sister insisted to her classmates that she was an only child; a subterfuge that became increasingly difficult to maintain as genetic look-alikes began roaming the high school halls. While this teenage dagger struck briefly at the heart, it was readily forgotten years later when this same sibling faced a life threatening illness and her sisters gathered quickly around.

So this collection of quotations is not intended to be blemish-free. For every human bond, inspirational books abound. But sisters cannot be so neatly categorized. The bonds of sisterhood are life-long, and consequently, much richer than non-sisters would ever suspect. Like sisters themselves, this gathering offers a loving and nasty dose of recognition.

–Maureen Slattery

An Everlasting Bond

Whose loves
Are dearer than the natural bond of sisters.

—SHAKESPEARE, As You Like It

If we believed in the media we would think the only significant relationship in our lives is a romantic one. Yet sisterhood is probably the one that will last longer than any other...a sister will always be around.

—JANE DOWDESWELL

Yet still my fate permits me this relief,
To write to lovely Delia all my grief,
To you alone I venture to complain;
From others hourly strive to hide my pain.

—ABIGAIL COLMAN DENNIE,
letter to her sister Jane Colman

You can't think how I depend on you, and when you're not there the color goes out of my life as water from a sponge; and I merely exist, dry and dusty.

—VIRGINIA WOOLF, letter to her sister Vanessa Bell

There can be no situation in life in which the conversation of my dear sister will not administer some comfort to me.

—LADY MARY WORTLEY MONTAGU

Whom still I've hungered after more than bread,
My sister Marian?—can I hurt thee, dear?
Then why distrust me? Never tremble so.
Come with me rather, where we'll talk and live,
And none shall vex us. I've a home for you
And me and no one else...

—ELIZABETH BARRETT BROWNING, *Aurora Leigh*

Few delights can equal the mere presence of one whom we trust utterly.

—GEORGE MACDONALD

So closely interwoven have been our lives, our purposes, and experiences that, separated, we have a feeling of incompleteness—united, such strength of self-associations that no ordinary obstacles, difficulties, or dangers ever appear to us insurmountable.

—ELIZABETH CADY STANTON
on her friendship with Susan B. Anthony

She'd tear off the ear of anyone who said an unkind word about me. That counts for a lot.

—AMY TAN

The two children were so fond of each other that they always held each other by the hand when they went out together, and when Snow-White said, "We will not leave each other," Rose-Red answered, "Never so long as we live," and their mother would add, "What one has she must share with the other."

—The Brothers Grimm,
"Snow-White and Rose-Red"

Wherever I turn, in the house or out-of-doors, I seem to see your face before my eyes, and when I find myself deceived, and realize that you are really gone, you will understand how sore my distress has been—nay, how great it still is.

—Beatrice d'Este,
letter to her sister Isabella d'Este

I feel shelter to speak to you.

—Emily Dickinson, letter to her sister

Oh the comfort, the inexpressible comfort of feeling safe with a person: having neither to weigh thoughts nor measure words, but to pour them out.

—GEORGE ELIOT

So, when parted, Edith spoke no word,
She wept no tear, but round my Evelyn clung
In utter silence for so long, I thought
"What, will she never set her sister free?"

—ALFRED LORD TENNYSON, "The Sisters"

By slight indications the sisters could convey much to each other.

—E. M. FORSTER, *Howard's End*

One sister have I in our house,
And one a hedge away.
There's only one recorded
But both belong to me.

—EMILY DICKINSON, "The Single Hound"

Lord help the mister who comes between me
    and my sister
And Lord help the sister who comes between
    me and my man.

—IRVING BERLIN, "Sisters, Sisters"

I have lost such a sister, such a friend as can never have been surpassed...I had not a thought concealed from her and it is as if I had lost part of myself.

—CASSANDRA AUSTEN on her sister Jane

"Johnny, my child, take care of your only sister, Sally; for she's the brightest gem that ever sparkled on your early brow."

—CHARLES DICKENS,
The Haunted Man and The Ghost's Bargain

We are family
I got all my sisters with me
We are family
Get up everybody and sing.

—Sister Sledge, "We Are Family"

But he thought of his sisters, proud and cold,
And his mother, vain of her rank and gold.

—John Greenleaf Whittier

More important than anything is having your sister with you when there is family suffering. It divides the pain and trouble in half when you carry the burden together.

—Catherine Glackin

Sibling Rivalry

Sisters is probably the most competitive relationship within the family, but once sisters are grown, it becomes the strongest relationship.

—MARGARET MEAD

My sister and I never engaged in sibling rivalry. Our parents weren't crazy about either one of us.

—ERMA BOMBECK

The rod produces an effect which terminates in itself. A child is afraid of being whipped, and gets his task, and there's an end on 't; whereas, by exciting emulations and comparisons of superiority, you lay the foundation of lasting mischief; you make brothers and sisters hate each other.

—SAMUEL JOHNSON

Never praise a sister to a sister, in the hope of your compliments reaching the proper ears... Sisters are women first, and sisters afterwards; and you will find that you do yourself harm.

—RUDYARD KIPLING, "False Dawn"

Best masters for the young writer and speaker are the fault-finding brothers and sisters at home who will not spare him, but will pick and cavil, and tell the odious truth.

—RALPH WALDO EMERSON

The woman is so hard
Upon the woman.

—ALFRED LORD TENNYSON, "The Princess"

Hell hath no fury like a woman scorned... especially in favor of her sister.

—JOAN FONTAINE

When the wedding with the King's son had to be celebrated, the two false sisters came and wanted to get into favour with Cinderella and share her good fortune. When the betrothed couple went to church, the elder was at the right side and the younger at the left, and the pigeons pecked out one eye of each of them.

—THE BROTHERS GRIMM, "Cinderella"

Fighting is essentially a masculine idea; a woman's weapon is her tongue.

—HERMIONE GINGOLD

Sisters define their rivalry in terms of competition for the gold cup of parental love. It is never perceived as a cup which runneth over, rather a finite vessel from which the more one sister drinks, the less is left for the others.

—ELIZABETH FISHEL

If you don't understand how a woman could both love her sister dearly and want to wring her neck at the same time, then you were probably an only child.

—LINDA SUNSHINE

Of the two sisters, I loved the young.
With sensitive instincts, she was the creative one.

—BOB DYLAN, "Ballad in Plain D"

I had been a new experience for my parents: my sister found it much more difficult to surprise and astonish them; I had never been compared with anyone: she was always being compared with me.

—SIMONE DE BEAUVOIR,
Memoirs of a Dutiful Daughter

Comparison is the death knell to sibling harmony.

—ELIZABETH FISHEL

'Boud, Debo and I were too uncomfortably close in age for friendship. We got dreadfully in each other's way in the fierce and competitive struggle to grow up.

—JESSICA MITFORD

Near or far, there are burdens and terrors in sisterhood.

—HELEN YGLESIAS, *Family Feeling*

It is said that nothing gives a brighter glow to the complexion, or makes the eyes of a beautiful woman sparkle so intensely, as triumph over another.

—LADY CAROLINE LAMB

The young ladies entered the drawing-room in the full fervor of sisterly animosity.

—R. S. SURTEES, *Mr. Sponge's Sporting Tour 1853*

To both these sisters have I sworn my love;
Each jealous of the other, as the stung
Are of the adder.

—SHAKESPEARE, *King Lear*

The two sisters were like a pair of scissors snipping off everything that came athwart them; of like a knife and a whetstone, the one sharpened against the other.

—D. H. LAWRENCE, *Women in Love*

"To hell with sisters," said Beryl. "Give 'em all a good swift kick in the pants."

—JANE BOWLES, "Camp Cataract"

The empty woman took toys!
In her sisters' homes
Were little girls and boys.

—GWENDOLYN BROOKS

From the moment the two sisters met, I was no longer a free man. They enslaved me with their love for me, their love towards each other, and their jealousy. One minute they would be kissing and crying from devotion and suddenly they would begin to slug away, pull hair, and curse each other with words you wouldn't hear in the underworld.

—Isaac Bashevis Singer, "A Tale of Two Sisters"

But when my two sisters saw me with the young man, they envied me on his account, and malevolently plotted against me.

—"The Story of the First of the Three Ladies of Baghdad," *The Thousand and One Nights*

Marcia, Marcia, Marcia.

—Jan, *The Brady Bunch*

A Sister's Love

For there is no friend like a sister
In calm or stormy weather;
To cheer one on the tedious way,
To fetch one if one goes astray,
To lift one if one totters down,
To strengthen whilst one stands.

—CHRISTINA ROSSETTI, "Goblin Market"

I could never love anyone as I love my sisters.

—LOUISA MAY ALCOTT, Jo in *Little Women*

Is solace anywhere
more comforting
than that in the arms
of sisters?

—ALICE WALKER, "Telling"

There is no substitute for the comfort supplied by the utterly taken-for-granted relationship.

—Iris Murdoch

You know full as well as I do the value of sisters' affections to each other; there is nothing like it in this world.

—Charlotte Brontë

And yet at the same time it seemed to absolve a whole area of human relationship, to rescue it, wholesale, from the scruffy ragbag of the tag ends of family bitterness and domestic conflict. And such affection had, surely, its precedents, for were not sisters classically intended to love, and not despise one another?

—Margaret Drabble, *Jerusalem the Golden*

I came to the time when I first saw my dear girl
and was received into that sisterly affection which
was the grace and beauty of my life.

—CHARLES DICKENS, *Bleak House*

The love expressed between women is particular
and powerful, because we have had to love in
order to live; love has been our survival.

—AUDRE LORDE

Ah, how good and perfect you have been to me,
you—my own beloved sisters—heart and eyes over-
flow when I think of you!

—ELIZABETH BARRETT BROWNING

Letty and I are just one of those things that are
luck. I liked her from the moment I met her.

—WOODY ALLEN on his sister Letty

Sisterhood is to friendship what an arranged marriage is to romance. You are thrown together for life, no questions asked (until later), no chance of escape. And if you're lucky, you find love despite the confinement.

—LISA GRUNWALD

In thee my soul shall own combined
The sister and the friend.

If from my eyes by thee detained
    The wanderer cross the seas,
No more thy love shall soothe, as friend,
    No more as sister please.

—CATHERINE KILLIGREW, "Untitled"

Why does she feel that I'm the most important person in her life?—the most! Why does she say over and over again that even if we were not sisters, she would feel this way?

—AMY TAN, *The Hundred Secret Senses*

A ministering angel shall my sister be.

—SHAKESPEARE, *Hamlet*

My sister! my sweet sister! if a name Dearer and purer were, it should be thine

—LORD BYRON, "Epistle to Augusta"

My sister! With that thrilling word.
Let thoughts unnumbered wildly spring!
What echoes in my heart are stirred,
While thus I touch the trembling string.

—MARGARET DAVIDSON,
"To My Mother, Oppressed with Sorrow"

A man with six sisters, Spider realized with glee, was a rich man—unless he was Greek and had a duty to marry them off.

—JUDITH KRANTZ, *Scruples*

I cannot heave
My heart into my mouth. I love your Majesty
According to my bond; no more nor less.

—SHAKESPEARE, *King Lear*

Surely a gentle sister is the second best gift to a man; and it is first in point of occurrence; for the wife comes after.

—HERMAN MELVILLE

The angel of the Family is Woman. Mother, wife, or sister, Woman is the caress of life, the soothing sweetness of affection shed over its toils, a reflection for the individual of the loving providence which watches over Humanity.

—GIUSEPPE MAZZINI

Come, my sister,
we are two virgins,
our lives once more perfected
and unused.

—ANNE SEXTON, "Walking in Paris"

Difference and Repetition

And the first thing I do when I open my eyes is smile, and then I say, "Thank you, Lord, for another day!" If I don't hear Bessie get up, I'll go to her room and wake her. Sometimes I have to knock on her headboard. And she opens her eyes and says, "Oh, Lord, another day?"

—SARAH DELANY

But that is one great difference between us. Compliments always take you by surprise, and me never.

—JANE AUSTEN, *Pride and Prejudice*

Mrs. Ludlow was the eldest of the three sisters, and was usually thought the most sensible; the classification being in general that Lilian was the practical one, Edith the beauty, and Isabel the "Intellectual" one.

—HENRY JAMES, *The Portrait of a Lady*

Molly my sister and I fell out,
And what do you think it was all about?
She loved coffee and I loved tea,
And that was the reason we couldn't agree.

—MOTHER GOOSE

MICKEY: I don't understand you—your sister,
   both sisters, have such good taste in music.
   I don't know where you went wrong.
HOLLY: Do you mind? I'm my own person.

—WOODY ALLEN, *Hannah and Her Sisters*

It's the good girls who keep the diaries; the bad
girls never have the time.

—TALLULAH BANKHEAD

Siblings either learn to accept one another as independent individuals with their own sets of values and behaviors or cling to the shadow of the brother and sister they once knew.

—Jane Mersky Leder

These were calamitous sisters, ambitious sisters, sisters who stood by the window at night weeping over the moon; they were sisters who cut out advertisements from the newspapers for pretty dresses and sat in front of an old foot-pedaled Singer sewing machine making lace bonnets and lace-trimmed dresses.

—Oscar Hijuelos,
The Fourteen Sisters of Emilio Montez O'Brien

She was open, ardent, and not in the least self-admiring; indeed, it was pretty to see how her imagination adorned her sister Celia with attractions superior to her own, and if any gentleman appeared to come to the Grange from some other motive than that of seeing Mr. Brooke, she concluded that he must in love with Celia.

—GEORGE ELIOT, *Middlemarch*

Of two sisters
One is always the watcher,
One the dancer.

—LOUISE GLÜCK, "Descending Figure"

I always wanted to be like you. And care passionately about things. But I don't. I don't know why, but I don't. You've always had these strong feelings about things. I could feel strongly about your cheeseburger, however.

—SUSANNA MOORE, *The Whiteness of Bones*

Two girls there are: within the house
One sits; the other, without.
Daylong a duet of shade and light
Plays between these.

—Sylvia Plath, "Two Sisters of Persephone"

Since they could remember, there had been a mixture of criticism and awe in the attitude of Celia's mind towards her elder sister. The younger had always worn a yoke; but is there any yoked creature without its private opinions?

—George Eliot, *Middlemarch*

I'm a single careerist with a master's degree and walk-up apartment in New York; she's a married, pregnant, dog-owning baker in Montana with a, swear to God, white picket fence. People love that about us, love that I can't sew on a button but she makes quilts.

—Sarah Vowell

Dad was cruelest to Myrtle, who was rebellious, daring, openly disobedient, always under the threat of being sent to the industrial school at Caversham, whereas I who wanted only to be "good" and approved of, was timidly obedient except where I could deceive with a certainty of not being caught.

—JANET FRAME, *To the Is-Land*

Little sister, don't you kiss me once or twice
Then say it's very nice
And then you run
Little sister, don't you
Do what your big sister done

—ELVIS PRESLEY, "Little Sister"

I guess I've always been the sister who's a little bit of a renegade—which must be why my apartment is so small.

—SHEILA DOLAN of The Satellite Sisters

"I have never felt like Isabel's sister, and I am sure I never shall," she had said to an intimate friend; a declaration which made it all the more creditable that she had been prolific in sisterly offices.

—HENRY JAMES, *The Portrait of a Lady*

Younger sisters are almost different beings from elder ones, but thank God it is quite and unaffectedly without repining or envy that I see my elder sister gad about and visit, etc.—when I rest at home.

—FANNY BURNEY

Just because we're sisters under the skin doesn't mean we've got much in common.

—ANGELA CARTER

Sisterhood

Helping one another is part of the religion of our sisterhood.

—Louisa May Alcott, *An Old Fashioned Girl*

It is only the women whose eyes have been washed clear with tears who get the broad vision that makes them little sisters to all the world.

—Dorothy Dix

Am I not a woman and a sister?

—"Ladies Department," *The Liberator*

Before any woman is a wife, a sister or a mother she is a human being. We ask nothing as women but everything as human beings.

—Ida C. Hultin

We might join hands with women who are, after all, our sisters and together imagine a world whose subsequent creation would lead to the need for a new fantasy altogether.

—Janice A. Radway

Sisters are doin' it for themselves.
Standin' on their own two feet.
And ringin' on their own bells.
Sisters are doin' it for themselves.

—Annie Lennox

Sisterhood is Powerful.

—Robin Morgan

Women are the architects of society.

—Harriet Beecher Stowe

When you get to a man in the case,
They're like as a row of pins—
For the Colonel's Lady an' Judy O'Grady
Are sisters under their skins!

—RUDYARD KIPLING, "The Ladies"

People are just not very ambitious for women still. Your son you want to be the best he can be. Your daughter you want to be happy.

—ALEXA CANADY

For older sisters are very sobering things.
Put on your cloaks, my dears, the motor's waiting.
No, you have not seemed strange to me, but near
Frightfully near, and rather terrifying.

—AMY LOWELL, "The Sisters"

I forged the thunderbolts; she fired them.

—ELIZABETH CADY STANTON
on her friendship with Susan B. Anthony

Alone we can do so little; together we can do so much.

—HELEN KELLER

All the brothers were valiant, and all the sisters virtuous.

—Inscription on the DUCHESS OF NEWCASTLE'S
tomb in Westminster Abbey

Little sister, the sky is falling,
I don't mind, I don't mind.
Little sister, the fates are calling on you.

—PATTI SMITH, "Kimberly"

Not the man's nation only, but the woman's nation—a land of splendid mothers, daughters, sisters, wives.

—WALT WHITMAN

Sisters, I a'n't clear what you'd be after. Ef women want any rights more'n dey's got, why don't dey jes take 'em, an' not be talkin' about it?

—SOJOURNER TRUTH

To become a token woman—whether you win the Nobel Prize or merely get tenure at the cost of denying your sisters—is to become something less than a man . . . since men are loyal at least to their own world-view, their laws of brotherhood and self-interest.

—ADRIENNE RICH

I write mainly for the kindly race of women. I am their sister, and in no way exempt from their sorrowful lot. I have drank the cup of their limitations to the dregs, and if my experience can help any sad or doubtful woman to outleap her own shadow, and to stand bravely out in the sunshine to meet her destiny, whatever it may be, I shall have done well; I have not written this book in vain.

—AMELIA E. BARR

It's babe feminism—we're young, we're fun, we do what we want in bed—and it has a shorter shelf life than the feminism of sisterhood. I've been a babe, and I've been a sister. Sister lasts longer.

—Anna Quindlen

Famous Sisters

It is true that I was born in Iowa, but I can't speak for my twin sister.

—ABIGAIL VAN BUREN (DEAR ABBY)
on her sister Ann Landers

I felt Olivia would spring across the table and grab me by my hair. I felt aged four, being confronted by my older sister…It was a bittersweet moment. I was appalled that I'd won over my sister.

—JOAN FONTAINE on winning the Oscar
over her sister Olivia de Haviland

We know at least that all the Brontë virgins, Charlotte, Anne, and Emily, loved with brute passion, committed adultery and incest, bore illegitimate children, moldered in dungeons, murdered, revenged, conquered, and died unrepentant in the imaginary kingdoms they called Gondal and Angria.

—ELLEN MOERS

We were a club, a society, a civilization all our own.

—ANNETTE, CÉCILE, EMILIE, MARIE,
and YVONNE DIONNE

And you were afraid that people would think something was wrong with us because we don't argue. So you told the reporter we fight over normal sister things. And me, Ms. Blunt Louise, said, "No, we don't," and right there we had our first argument—over whether or not we argue.

—LOUISE MANDRELL
on her sisters Barbara and Irlene

The career thing is just a blip. Maybe our songs will go on. Maybe not. But this sister thing we have will go on as long as we live.

—ANNA MCGARRIGLE on
The McGarrigle Sisters, folksingers

Poor Margaret, I do understand. It is easy to tolerate in one's sister those emotions we suppress in ourselves.

—QUEEN ELIZABETH on her sister Princess Margaret

Liza would get up and sing and sing and sing. I would ask to sing. Mama would insist I go out of the room and make a proper entrance. When I came back, everybody would be gone.

—LORNA LUFT on her sister Liza Minnelli

Delia really can say virtually anything to me and I'm afraid she often does.

—NORA EPHRON on her sister Delia

We make a good team, we knock heads, we have our knock-down-drag-outs, but then we pick each other up and walk off together.

—PHYLICIA RASHAD on her sister Debbie Allen

I can't pinpoint exactly when I stopped being daddy's little darling; it could have been when little baby Jackie arrived to take some of the attention away from me.

—JOAN COLLINS on her sister Jackie

I just have to say it happened last summer, when I was on tour with Nancy, and I can't think of one moment, but it was just the musical ecstasy we had going last summer.

—ANN WILSON on her sister Nancy and their band Heart

She was up there supporting me. After I lost my first two match points, I looked over to—not my mom or dad, I saw them also—but I saw Venus over there really making sure, pumping me up. It really helped me.

—SERENA WILLIAMS on her sister Venus

And they filmed scenes that absolutely did not occur in real life, like me saying to my sister "I don't hate you, but you got Mom—I envy you." The three of us were watching it, and I just had a fit, totally exploded.

—Ashley Judd on her sister Wynnona

The popular conception of Lillian as soft and dreamy makes me think a little of the "gag" used too often in the comic strips. A hat lies upon the sidewalk; some person kicks it enthusiastically and finds to his astonishment and pain that there is hidden inside it a brick.

—Dorothy Gish on her sister Lillian

Nancy: Sisters are a defense against life's cruel circumstances.
Jessica: Sisters are life's cruel circumstances.

—Nancy and Jessica Mitford

All eyes and all attention were on Jackie. We had always done everything together, but now we were separated and I felt frantic.

—HILARY DU PRÉ on her sister Jacqueline

Our family really does enjoy being together, seeing each other's work. We rejoice in each other's achievements and try to be philosophical about our failures or setbacks. I adore and admire my sister Lynn.

—VANESSA REDGRAVE on her sister Lynn

She gets up in the morning, and goes through all the newspapers looking for her name and if she doesn't find it, she just throws them all away, and when she sees her name, she cuts it out immediately!

—LEE RADZIWELL on her sister
Jacqueline Kennedy Onassis

I stopped reading movie magazines in the beauty parlor a couple of years ago because I could not accommodate any more information about something called the Lennon Sisters.

—Nora Ephron

Our Sisters,
Our Selves

Both within the family and without, our sisters hold up our mirrors: our images of who we are and of who we can dare to be.

—ELIZABETH FISHEL

I cannot deny that, now I am without your company I feel not only that I am deprived of a very dear sister, but that I have lost half of myself.

—BEATRICE D'ESTE, letter to her sister

By now we anticipate one another so easily, so deeply, we unthinkingly finish each other's sentences, and often speak in code. No one else knows what I mean so exquisitely, painfully well; no one else knows so exactly what to say, to fix me.

—JOAN FRANK

Your sister is the only creature on earth who shares your heritage, history, environment, DNA, bone structure, and contempt for stupid Aunt Gertie.

—LINDA SUNSHINE

Sisters we are, yea, twins we be,
Yet deadly feud 'twixt thee and me;
For from one father are we not,
Thou by old Adam wast begot,
But my arise is from above

—ANNE BRADSTREET, "The Flesh and the Spirit"

My sister and I may have been crafted of the same genetic clay, baked in the same uterine kiln, but we were disparate species, doomed never to love each other except blindly.

—JUDITH KELMAN, *Where Shadows Fall*

A sibling may be the sole keeper of one's core identity, the only person with the keys to one's unfettered, more fundamental self.

—MARIAN SANDMAIER

And lovelier things have mercy shown
To every failing but their own;
And every woe a tear can claim,
Except an erring sister's shame.

—LORD BYRON, "The Giaour"

Together we look like our mother. Her same eyes, her same mouth, open in surprise to see, at last, her long-cherished wish.

—AMY TAN

I miss the way I was never Sarah and my sister was never Amy, but we were together AmyandSarah. Unlike the identicals, who act as photocopies of each other, we're fraternal. Which means that we're not doubles so much as halves; we're split down the middle.

—SARAH VOWELL

After so long, we are in some ways like one person. She is my right arm.

—SADIE DELANY

Your sister is your other self. She is your alter ego, your reflection, your foil, your shadow.

—BARBARA MATHIS

Sisters are always drying their hair.
Locked into rooms, alone,
They pose at the mirror, shoulders bare,
Trying this way and that their hair,
Or fly importunate down the stair
To answer the telephone.

—PHYLLIS MCGINLEY

So important, in fact, is the role that sisters play in cementing family ties that some families all but fall apart without them.

—ERICA E. GOODE

Family is just accident…They don't mean to get on your nerves. They don't even mean to be your family, they just are.

—MARSHA NORMAN, *'night Mother*

Sometimes it seems as if, when our parents created us, it took them two tries, two daughters, to get all the qualities of one whole, well-put-together person.

—Lois Lowry, A Summer to Die

Behind your fiery make-up you should know this I am your sister, I am your kin, your flesh and kin.

—Joan Baez, "The Hitchhiker's Song"

When they were together, doing the things they enjoyed, the two sisters were quite complete in a perfect world of their own.

—D. H. Lawrence, Women in Love

I owe a great debt to my sister for helping me to externalize many of my dreams in play: she also helped me to save my daily life from silence; through her I got into the habit of wanting to communicate with people.

—SIMONE DE BEAUVOIR,
Memoirs of a Dutiful Daughter

All three sisters had the same high-bridged noses...I pored over these pictures, intrigued by the idea of the triplicate, identical noses. I did not have a sister myself, then, and the mystique of sisterhood was potent for me.

—MARGARET ATWOOD

Brothers and sisters were a mystery to her. There were Grace and Vera, speaking like two mouths out of the same head, and Wilfred and Albert without a thread of connection between them.

—ALICE MUNRO

We are each other's reference point at our turning points.

—ELIZABETH FISHEL

The daughters never were
True brides of the father

The daughters were to begin with
Brides of the mother

Then brides of each other
Under a different law

Let me hold and tell you

—ADRIENNE RICH, "Sibling Mysteries"

There is nowhere I shall not drag this grotesque shadow, our joint creature. I can choose, at least, to put out the light that throws it. I want no more reflections.

—A. S. BYATT, *The Game*

Take away my sisters, and there is very little of me left…And certainly no heart for living.

—Keri Hulme, "I Aim Carefully"

My sister and I, you will recollect, were twins, and you know how subtle are the links which bind two souls which are so closely allied.

—Sir Arthur Conan Doyle

Evelyn Mulwray: She's my daughter.
J.J. Gittes: I said I want the truth!
Evelyn Mulwray: She's my sister. She's my daughter. My sister, my daughter.
J.J. Gittes: I said I want the truth!
Evelyn Mulwray: She's my sister and my daughter!

—Robert Towne, *Chinatown*

Sister
Girlfriends

I realize how sweet and slippery is this word "sister"—big enough to stretch beyond biology and across time; flexible enough to define soul mates and virtual strangers; precise enough to embrace me and [my two sisters], my two daughters, and all the sisterhoods in between.

—LETTY COTTIN POGREBIN

Being in this band [the Spice Girls] is like having four (three now) older sisters. They all look after me and I couldn't dream of leaving them.

—EMMA BUNTON (Baby Spice)

It's the ones you can call up at 4 A.M. that matter.

—MARLENE DIETRICH

she was the only friend I had cd read me
like a miles davis solo
she was like a sister

—N<small>TOZAKE</small> S<small>HANGE</small>

It seems to me that trying to live without friends
is like milking a bear to get cream for your morning coffee. It is a whole lot of trouble, and then
not worth much after you get it.

—Z<small>ORA</small> N<small>EALE</small> H<small>URSTON</small>

Constant use had not worn ragged the fabric of
their friendship.

—D<small>OROTHY</small> P<small>ARKER</small>

She is a friend of my mind. She gathers me, man. The pieces I am, she gather them and give them back to me in all the right order. It's good, you know, when you got a woman who is a friend of your mind.

—TONI MORRISON, *Beloved*

Consider the friendships between girl children. The intricacies of Mideast diplomacy are not as tangled as the negotiations, counteractions, and introspections that go on between "best friends" of the female persuasion.

—NANCY MOSER

Little gal, no matter what people say or do, no matter what happens, you and me are gonna stick together.

—PATSY CLINE to Loretta Lynn

The real marriage of true minds is for any two people to possess a sense of humor or irony pitched in exactly the same key, so that their joint glances at any subject cross like interarching searchlights.

—EDITH WHARTON, *A Backward Glance*

Intimacies between women often go backwards, beginning in revelations and ending up in small talk without loss of esteem.

—ELIZABETH BOWEN, *The Death of the Heat*

Though friendship is not quick to burn, It is explosive stuff.

—MAY SARTON

We frequently would dial one another in the morning and stay connected all day... It was not unusual for us to have the phone down on the desk and each be going about our day doing other things, and whistle into the phone when we wanted the other one.

—MAXINE KUMIN on Anne Sexton

Once Zaki and I were jumping up and down singing with the TV, and her mother shook her head and said, "I know because I was there that you all came out of different wombs, but I swear that you came out at the same time."

—THULANI on Ntozake (Zaki) Shange

Any deep relationship to another human being requires watchfulness and nourishment; otherwise it is taken from us. And we cannot recapture it. This is a form of having and not having that is the root of innumerable tragedies.

—PAUL TILLICH

The only two adult females we know who enjoyed this sort of friendship were almost certainly sisters; not only did they look alike facially, but they had the same massive build, and both were prone to perform charging displays, stamping on the ground and swaggering in manner more typical of males.

—JANE GOODALL, *In the Shadow of Man*

I think he suspects that he will never be as essential to me as you and the Ya-Yas. We have to keep these men in the dark, you know, or the whole world would fall to pieces.

—REBECCA WELLS,
The Divine Secrets of the Ya-Ya Sisterhood

And we became a team, best friends through junior high, high school and into college. Twins separated at birth—identical in size—one with a beautiful Irish face, the other a Jewish girl with a ponytail.

—JUDY BLUME, *Summer Sisters*

God gave us our relatives—thank God we can choose our friends.

—ETHEL WATTS MUMFORD

Growing Up

Hallie and I...were all there was. The image in the mirror that proves you are still here. We had exactly one sister apiece. We grew up knowing the simple arithmetic of scarcity: A sister is more precious than an eye.

—BARBARA KINGSOLVER, *Animal Dreams*

My sister, four years older, simply existed for me because I had to sleep in the same room with her. Besides, it is natural not to care about a sister, certainly not when she is four years older and grinds her teeth at night.

—GERTRUDE STEIN, *Everybody's Autobiography*

Who told my mother of my same,
Who told my father of my dear?
Oh who but Maude, my sister Maude,
Who lurked to spy and peer.

—CHRISTINA ROSSETTI, "Sister Maude"

A baby sister is nicer than a goat. You'll get used to her.

—LYNN ALPERN AND ESTHER BLUMENFELD

Mama came from a family of many sisters. And she preached to us endlessly about the necessity of living in harmony with one another.

—BELL HOOKS

My sister taught me everything I need to know, and she was only in the sixth grade at the time.

—LINDA SUNSHINE

My fear was that, once married, my sisters would turn their backs on the family, choosing to spend their vacations and holidays with their husbands. One by one, they would abandon us until it was just me and my parents eating our turkey and stuffing off TV trays. It wasn't difficult getting the signatures. The girls in my family didn't play house, they played reformatory.

—DAVID SEDARIS

Mamie had learned long ago that Claire saw things in a way altogether different from her own view, so Mamie was always very interested to hear Claire's version of things. She questions Claire ceaselessly about the past, not because she required pure information, nor to reinforce her own cool, fastidious memory, but because the variations in the story thrilled her.

—SUSANNA MOORE, *The Whiteness of Bones*

Even where the affections are not strongly moved by any superior excellence, the companions of our childhood always possess a certain power over our minds which hardly any later friend can obtain.

—MARY SHELLEY, *Frankenstein*

I was tired of sharing a room with the baby (Lian) and tired of sharing a room with a sister who constantly teased me (Sheila) and tired of sharing a room with a chronic sleepwalker who was always banging into the furniture at night (Liz).

—MONICA DOLAN of The Satellite Sisters

"Why did you beat me up so much when we were little?" I ask my sister.
"What did you do that made me?" she replies.

—PATRICIA VOLK

I was sorry for children who had no brother or sister; solitary amusements seemed insipid to me; no better than a means of killing time. But when there were two, hopscotch or a ball game were adventurous undertakings, and bowling hoops an exciting competition.

—SIMONE DE BEAUVOIR,
Memoirs of a Dutiful Daughter

Big sisters are the crabgrass on the lawn of life.

—LINUS, *Peanuts*

Once I saw Luther and Johnny sharing the same frame, it hit me how much they have in common with my sister and me. The similarities are uncanny. Luther and Johnny are illiterate, Baptist, messianic insurgents struggling against the government of Myanmar, and my sister Amy and I shared a locker all through junior high.

—SARAH VOWELL

You see I'd never be like Sis is now. I wouldn't. Anybody could know that if they knew me. I just wouldn't, that's all. I don't want to grow up—if it's like that.

—CARSON MCCULLERS, "Like That"

You would run and dance across the field
    and hay
I would hide behind to see where you would
    go to play
You were being Isadora
I was being you

—HOLLY NEAR, "You've Got Me Flying"

Above all, perhaps, sisters who have grown up close to one another know how their daydreams have been interwoven with their life experiences.

—MARGARET MEAD, *Blackberry Winter*

Adulthood was invented to repair the wounds of childhood.

—Joy Brown

Each of the sisters, as she came up for the first time to the surface of the water, was delighted with the new and beautiful sights she saw; but as they now had permission, as grown-up girls, to go whenever they liked, it became indifferent to them. They wished themselves back again, and after a month had elapsed they said it was best of all down below, for there one felt so comfortably at home.

—Hans Christian Anderson, *The Little Sea-maid*

Anne: He hit me, Jack. My own brother, he hit me.
Jack: Your brother's an old-fashioned man, he believes in a sister's honor. Me, I'm a Modern Man, the 20th-century type. I run.

—Robert Rossen, *All the King's Men*

Is all the counsel that we two have shared,
The sisters' vows, the hours that we have spent
When we have chid the hasty-footed time
For parting us—O, is all forgot?
All schooldays' friendship, childhood innocence?

—SHAKESPEARE, *A Midsummer Night's Dream*

Through the Years

Husbands come and go; children come and eventually they go. Friends grow up and move away. But the one thing that's never lost is your sister.

—Gail Sheehy

I've been a sister longer than I've been anything else in my life.

—Anna Quindlen

The love that grew with us from our cradles never knew diminution from time or distance. Other ties were formed, but they did not supersede or weaken this. Death tore away all that was mortal and perishable, but this tie he could not sunder.

—Charlotte Elizabeth Tonna

How this same little sister of hers would, in the after-time, be herself a grown woman; and how she would keep, through all her riper years, the simple and loving heart of her childhood.

—LEWIS CARROLL, *Alice's Adventures in Wonderland*

Often, in old age, they become each other's chosen and most happy companions. In addition to their shared memories of childhood and of their relationship to each other's children, they share memories of the same home, the same homemaking style, and the same small prejudices about housekeeping that carry the echoes of their mother's voice.

—MARGARET MEAD, *Blackberry Winter*

You keep your past by having sisters. As you get older they're the only ones who don't get bored if you talk about your memories . . .

—DEBORAH MOGGACH

What seems to us serious, significant and important will, in future times, be forgotten or won't seem important at all.

—Anton Chekhov, *The Three Sisters*

During that time at our mother's house my sisters were remote and mechanical, acting as though they were hotel maids tidying up after a stranger. They spoke as if a terrible chapter of their lives had just ended, and I felt alone in my belief that a much more terrible chapter was about to begin.

—David Sedaris

But she says my sister still calls every Sunday night
After the rates go down
And I still can never manage to say anything right

—Ani di Franco, "Jukebox"

Families will not be broken. Curse and expel them, send their children wandering, drown them in floods and fires, and old women will make songs out of all these sorrows and sit in the porches and sing them in mild evenings.

—Marilynne Robinson, *Housekeeping*

Oh, sister, when I come to knock on your door,
Don't turn away, you'll create sorrow.
Time is an ocean but it ends at the shore
You may not see me tomorrow.

—Bob Dylan, "Oh Sister"

And all that time their salvation was lying round them—the past sanctifying the present; the present with wild heart-throb, declaring that there would after all be a future with laughter and the voices of children. Helen, still smiling, came up to her sister. She said, "It is always Meg." They looked into each other's eyes. The inner life had paid.

—E. M. Forster, *Howard's End*

Nessa comes tomorrow—what one calls Nessa; but it means husband and baby; and of sister there is less than there used to be . . .

—VIRGINIA WOOLF on her sister Vanessa Bell

People change and forget to tell each other.

—LILLIAN HELLMAN

Sister I'm heading out of Alabama
So you better think fast . . .
Of where you've been and where you're going
    now.

—INDIGO GIRLS, "Sisters"

There is no one else on earth with whom you share so much personal history.

—JUDITH VIORST

After living these separate lives and finding independence, it was time to come back together as a family. I no longer wanted to be far apart from my brothers and sisters. When we reconnected, it was like having an instant circle of grown-up friends, but better because they could loan you money in a jam.

—MONICA DOLAN of The Satellite Sisters

To-day is far from childhood
But up and down the hills
I held her hand the tighter,
Which shortened all the miles.

—EMILY DICKINSON, "The Single Hound"

When we were kids, we took it for granted that there was always a sister on the other end of the teeter-totter. Now I realize what that really means. How do people get through life if they have to go to a playground by themselves?

—DONNA MASIEJCZYK

PK was the sister in the middle. There was one sister before her and one sister after. One above and one below. No matter what she did, she would always be stuck between them, right in the middle.

—SUSAN PATRON,
Maybe Yes, Maybe No, Maybe Maybe

On evenings when my grandmother's sisters sang; she had with this being, elsewhere so sought after, the naive roughness of a child who plays with a collector's item without any more care than with a less expensive one.

—MARCEL PROUST

The bell that tolls for a younger sister is much closer; its knell doesn't stop reverberating and it says, "You next. You next."

—JESSAMYN WEST

I have a fascinated glimpse of Maddy and myself, grown old, caught back in the web of sisterhood after everything else has disappeared, making tea for some young, loved, and essentially unimportant relative; what will anyone ever know of us?

—ALICE MUNRO, "The Peace of Utrecht"

Women and elephants never forget.

—DOROTHY PARKER